MAKE it WORK!

PLANTS

A Creative, Hands–On Approach to Science
Wendy Baker & Andrew Haslam

written by
Claire Watts and Alexandra Parsons

Photography: Jon Barnes
Series Consultant: John Chaldecott
Science Consultant: Bob Press
Professional Botanist

Aladdin Books   Macmillan Publishing Company   New York
Maxwell Macmillan International   New York   Oxford   Singapore   Sydney

MAKE it WORK!
Other titles

Earth
Electricity
Sound

First Aladdin Books edition 1993

First published in 1992 in Great Britain by Two-Can Publishing Ltd., London

Aladdin Books
Macmillan Publishing Company
866 Third Avenue
New York, NY 10022

Macmillan Publishing Company is part of the Maxwell Communications
Group of Companies.

Printed and bound in Hong Kong

10 9 8 7 6 5 4 3 2 1

Baker, Wendy.
  Plants: a creative, hands-on approach to science / written by Wendy Baker and
Andrew Haslam; [photography, Jon Barnes].—1st Aladdin Books ed.
     p.   cm.—(Make-it-work!)
  Includes index.
Summary: Experiments and other activities introduce plants and how they grow.
  ISBN: 0-689-71664-8
  1. Botany—Study and teaching—Activity programs—Juvenile literature. 2. Plants—
Experiments—Juvenile literature. [1. Botany—Experiments. 2. Plants—Experiments.
3. Experiments.] I. Haslam, Andrew. II. Barnes, Jon, ill. III. Title. IV. Series.
QK52.55.B36 1993
581'.078—dc20   92-24559

Editors: Claire Watts and Mike Hirst
Illustrator: Diana Leadbetter
Children's photography: Matthew Ward

Additional thanks to: Albert Baker, Catherine Bee, Tony Ellis,
Elaine Gardner, Nick Hawkins, Claudia Sebire and everyone at Plough Studios

Contents

Words marked in **bold** are explained in the glossary.

Scientists study the universe and the way it works. They study everything – from how the world began to the behavior of humans and to how plants grow. The study of plants is called **botany**. Botany is one branch of the science of **biology**, which is the study of all living things. Botanists study the structure of plants, their **environments**, and their uses.

MAKE it WORK!

In this book, you will explore the science of botany. As you follow the projects in the book, you will be investigating the plant world for yourself. To understand how a scientist works, it will be important to use scientific methods. For example, when you make observations, be as accurate as possible and label your **specimens** (your subjects) so you will be able to identify them later on.

Scientists use thorough, step-by-step methods to study their subjects carefully and record their observations accurately. They use observations to form **theories,** and test their theories by doing **experiments**. It may take many experiments before any definite answers are found.

▲ Use tweezers to handle specimens such as delicate flowers and seeds. Keep specimens sealed in plastic bags until you need them.

▶ Keep careful records throughout your experiments to refer to later on.

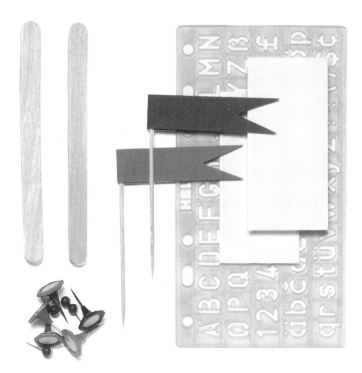

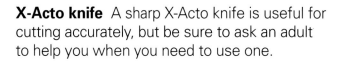

X-Acto knife
A sharp X-Acto knife is useful for cutting accurately, but be sure to ask an adult to help you when you need to use one.

Poster board
If possible, have different colored poster board available. Otherwise, you can paint plain poster board with poster paints.

Paper
Collect paper of different thicknesses and textures. Keep a pile of scratch paper to practice on. Reuse paper whenever you can.

Ruler
Use a ruler for making accurate measurements. A protractor and a T square may be helpful too.

▲ Always label things clearly so you can tell what they are.

You will need
The equipment you will need to do these projects is easy to find. You should be able to locate most of the things around the house or in an art supply store.

Glue
Use an all-purpose glue unless you are told otherwise. If you need a waterproof glue, rubber cement is best.

Scissors
Be careful when using scissors. Those with blunted ends are the safest type to use.

Cardboard
Collect thick and thin cardboard from old boxes and cartons.

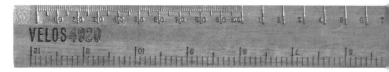

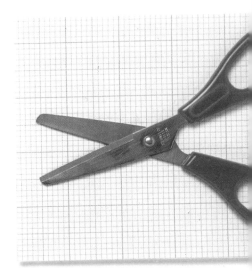

Botanists collect plant specimens to help study the plants more closely. By collecting, **cataloging**, and comparing natural objects, botanists try to discover differences and similarities between **species** of plants. The collection and study of such **data** is vital to all science.

MAKE it WORK!

Ask an adult to help you collect your own specimens. Try to collect things such as flowers, seeds, and nuts. Then make a box to display and store your collection.

You will need

thick poster board	glue or tape
ruler	toothpicks
pencil	Popsicle sticks
X-Acto knife	colored paper

1 Work out what size you want your box. Out of cardboard, cut out a flat shape like the one on the right.

2 Draw lines on your box to mark the exact position where the dividers will go.

tissue paper

cotton wool

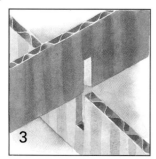

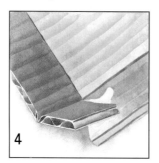

3 Make the dividers by cutting strips the same height as the box. Slot them together by cutting a slit halfway up one divider and half way down the other.

4 Fold up the sides of the box. Tuck in the corner flaps and glue or tape them in place. Push the dividers into place in the box.

sawdust

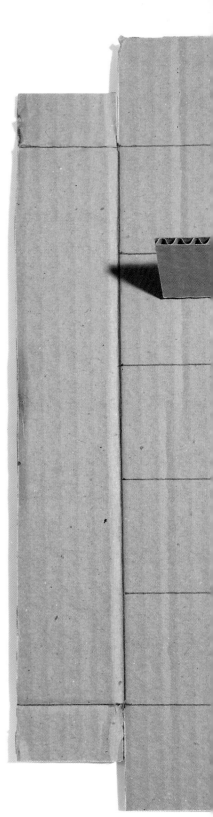

5 Fill the sections of the box with sawdust, cotton, or tissue paper before you add your collection.

The smallest plants in the world are diatoms. Because they can only be seen with a microscope, they are known as microorganisms. The world's largest plant is the giant sequoia tree from California. Some sequoias have grown to 335 feet tall, as high as a 30-story building.

Plants were the first forms of life on earth. Nonflowering plants appeared more than 570 million years ago. Early dinosaurs fed on giant tree ferns and gingko trees. Later, flowering plants, such as the magnolia, developed.

No one knows exactly how many species of plants there are in the world. There may be as many as 240,000 species of flowering plants alone. The other major plant groups are **ferns, conifers, lichens, mosses, algae,** and **fungi.**

Labeling

Sort your specimens into different categories such as seeds, flowers, and nuts. Try to find out the names of your specimens by looking for them in books or by asking other people. Label your specimens to help you identify them later on. To make the labels, write the specimens' names on Popsicle sticks or make flags from colored paper and toothpicks. Attach these labels to the different sections of the box with tape or glue. Try to find out the scientific names for your specimens and write these on the labels, too

In 1753, a Swedish botanist named Carolus Linnaeus invented a system of Latin names to classify the natural world. Plants are given a two-part name. The first part refers to the genus (or family) that the plant belongs to. The second part is the name of the species within that family. For example, the silver birch tree is called Betula pendula. Betula *is the birch tree and* pendula *is the species name.*

▼ Try making a double layer in one part of the box. Cut the dividers half the height of the box. Then use the same method as before to build a small, shallow tray to fit on top.

10 Growth

All healthy living things grow if they are given food, and plants are no exception. But unlike humans and animals, plants keep on growing all their lives. They make their own food from minerals and salts in the soil, and from sunlight and the gas **carbon dioxide**, which is found in air and water.

MAKE it WORK!

All plants and trees have to start somewhere. Huge oak trees were once acorns, and a field of ripe corn was once a sackful of seed. All it takes to make them grow is sunshine, water, and fertile soil. Experiment with three different ways to grow plants: from seed, from a bulb, and from a cutting. You can buy seeds and bulbs from a nursery or garden store. To make a cutting, cut a stalk off a healthy plant, just where it joins the main stem.

watercress seeds

sweet corn

broad beans

▲ Seeds come in all shapes and sizes.

You will need

a shallow dish	blotting paper
watercress seeds	small stones
potting soil	a bulb
a cutting from an existing plant	
two flower pots and saucers	
a glass of water	

1 To sow the watercress seeds: Cut a circle of blotting paper to fit the bottom of the shallow dish. Moisten it with water and sprinkle on the watercress seeds. Keep the blotting paper moist and watch for the watercress to sprout. When it gets tall enough, harvest your crop with scissors and sprinkle it on salads or in sandwiches.

▲ After two days, the watercress seeds will have swelled up and sent out curly shoots.

▲ After four days, little green leaves will have appeared. Soon it will be ready to eat.

daffodil bulb

hyacinth bulbs

2 To plant the bulb: Put a layer of small stones in the saucer of your plant pot – this is to help the water drain out of the pot so the bulb doesn't get waterlogged and soggy.

3 To root the cutting: Put the stem of the cutting into a glass of water. Check it every day, and when it begins to develop roots, plant it in potting soil. Water regularly.

Fill the plant pot with potting soil, and bury the bulb in the center. The pointed end of the bulb should be about a half inch below the surface of the soil.

Keep the soil moist and put the pot in a dark cupboard until a green shoot breaks through. Then bring it out into the light. Bulbs should be watered little but often.

Air is a mixture of oxygen, carbon dioxide, and two other gases. People take in oxygen and breathe out carbon dioxide. Plants take in carbon dioxide and give out oxygen.

12 Measuring Growth

Not all plants grow at the same rate. Some plants have a life cycle of only one year. For example, corn, which is sown after the winter frosts, starts to grow in spring, ripens in summer, and is ready for harvesting in the autumn. Other plants, particularly trees, take years to mature and keep on growing for centuries.

Most green plants grow in just two ways. They grow *up* from the tips of their stems and *down* from the tips of their roots. Woody plants like trees and shrubs grow up and down, too, but they also grow outward. Every year, they add a layer to their trunks, making them fatter.

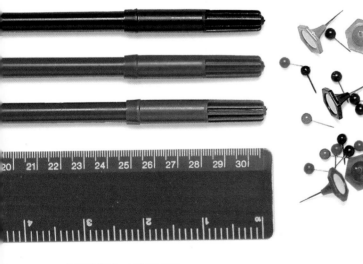

MAKE it WORK!
Plants grow because, like you, they have growth **hormones**. These hormones control the way a plant grows, making sure that roots go down and stems go up. This up-and-down growth is called primary growth, and width growth is known as secondary growth. Measure the primary growth of a houseplant and a watercress seed. Then measure a leaf to see how it spreads out as it grows.

You will need

ruler	poster board
wooden sticks	thumbtacks
glue	paint

Measuring root and stem growth

1 Make a measuring stick out of poster board. Using the ruler, mark it out in inches, starting with zero in the center and the measurements running out to both ends. The pointed end is going to be the root end.

2 Plant a batch of watercress, and take one seedling out each day to measure it. Place the seed on the zero and keep a record of the root growth on one side and the stem growth on the other.

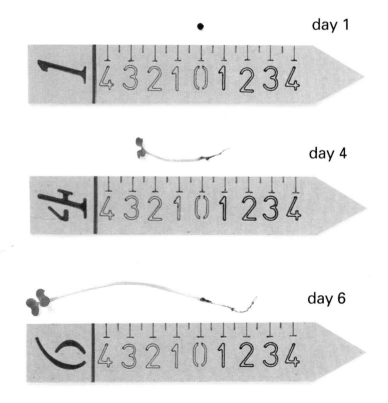

day 1

day 4

day 6

Many trees have a fairly short annual growing season – in the spring and summer. If a tree is cut down, you can see rings in the trunk, made by the different layers of growth each year. By counting the rings, you can tell how old the tree is.

Measuring stem growth

Take a young healthy houseplant and put a tall wooden stick into its pot. Make labels out of poster board and glue them onto the stick to mark the plant's growth. You can measure every week or every month, depending on the speed at which the plant grows.

Try measuring different types of plants. Do some grow more quickly than others?

Measuring leaf growth

1 This is a project for the springtime, when new leaves start their life cycle. Draw rules on a piece of graph paper, like the one above.

2 At regular intervals, take a leaf from the same tree. Using a large paintbrush, cover the leaf with thick paint.

3 Make a print of your leaf. (See more detailed explanation on pages 28-29.) When the paint has dried, cut around the leaf shape.

4 Glue your leaf print onto the poster board.

Most plants draw water from the ground up through their roots. Water travels up the stem of the plant into the leaves and flowers. Some of the water is used by the plant to make food, and some of it **evaporates** into the air through the surface of the leaves.

MAKE it WORK!

Here's a way to watch how water travels up the stems of plants. Try the experiment with different types of white flowers to see which ones work best. Try a stick of celery, too.

You will need

flowers	food coloring
glass containers	cardboard
water tape	celery

1 Fill several glass containers with water and add a different color food dye to each one. You probably will have to use quite a lot of dye to make the color dark enough for this experiment to work.

2 Place a flower in each container and leave it there while the stem sucks up the colored water.

3 Watch the flowers turn different colors as the water travels up the stems to reach them. It may take several hours or even a day.

▼ Make a multicolored flower! Split the stalk of one flower in two up the middle. Fill two glass containers with different-color dyes. Then place one half of the stalk in one vase and one half in the other.

Apart from sucking up water, roots also keep plants firmly anchored in the soil. Often, plants have more going on underground than above it.

Keeping a Record

Make a **calibrated** measuring stick, marking for both ounces and milliliters, out of poster board. Keep a record of how much water a plant absorbs over a period of time. Compare various flowers and plants: You will find that some are more "thirsty" than others.

```
200  7
     6
150  5
     4
100  3
     2
 50
     1
  0  0
    fl
ml  oz
```

▲ A cactus has very shallow, wide-spreading roots, but it also absorbs mist and dew through its spine.

Plants adapt to different climates in different parts of the world. Some places are hot and dry; others are cold and wet. But in almost every part of the world, there is some kind of plant life.

MAKE it WORK!

Bulrushes grow in wet marshes and mulga trees grow in the hot, dry Australian desert. Pine trees grow in snowbound forests and seaweed grows on the coast. Think of plants that grow in different environments and use them to play the environment game shown on the following pages.

You will need

colored poster board	glue
X-Acto knife	a pencil
graph paper	a ruler

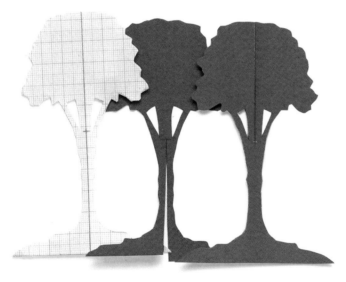

1 First make the plants. Choose four different environments and decide on a type of plant to use as a symbol of each environment. Trace the plant's shape twice onto colored poster board and cut out the two shapes. Make slits in the cutouts and slot them together so that the plants stand up. You should make four of each plant symbol. Use a different colored poster board for each type of plant.

2 Then make the board. On a large piece of poster board, draw twelve lines across and twelve lines down. Then cut some small squares out of colored poster board—thirteen each of red, yellow, black and blue. Lay them out to make a path around the board, like the one below. At each corner, stick on a "starting arrow."

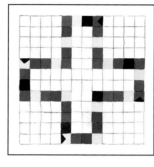 

3 Now make the four big environment corners for the board—one for each type of plant, in the same colours as the plants. Divide each corner into four big squares and sixteen smaller ones.

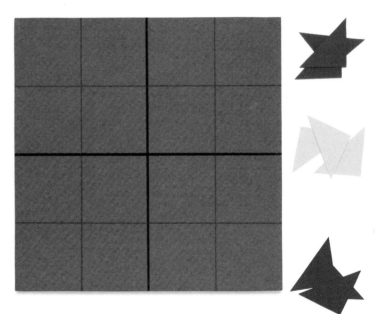

4 Make climate triangles—red represents heat, blue is water, and yellow is light. Glue these climate triangles onto the environment corners, to make the right environments for your plants. For instance, for a desert, use mostly red and yellow triangles: for a marshy riverside, use mainly blue and yellow ones.

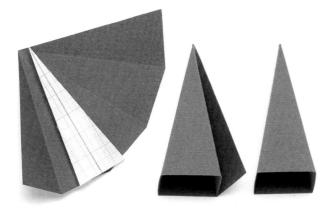

▼ You can use many different kinds of plants and environments to play this game.

Australian desert   **marsh**

5 Make the playing pieces. Each player needs three pyramids made from the same color poster board as his/her plants. Cut a triangle out of graph paper, making the base the same length as one of the squares on the board. Draw around the triangle five times, each time placing the long edges side by side. Then fold and glue the pyramid together, as shown above.

6 Finally, make climate pyramids to match your climate triangles. You need twelve of each in red, blue, and yellow. In the game, you will have to collect the right color climate pyramids needed to grow plants in your environment corner.

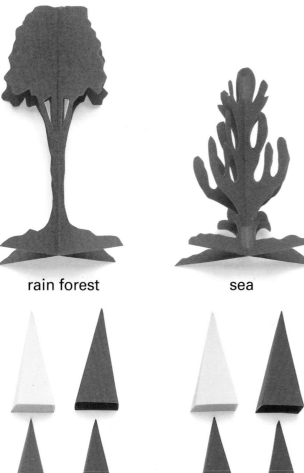

rain forest   **sea**   **coniferous forest**   **desert**

climate pyramids

Environment Game

The goal is to collect enough heat, light, and water to plant all four plants in your environment corner. But take care! If you land on a black square, you suffer an ecological disaster!

1 Players start the game with their three playing pieces on the starting arrow in their corner of the board. The blue, yellow, and red climate pyramids are stacked in the middle.

2 Players take turns by throwing the die and then moving any one of their three pieces clockwise around the board.

3 When a player lands on a colored square, he/she picks up a pyramid of that color and puts it on one of the matching climate squares. When the four climate squares that make up a section are covered, the player puts the pyramids back in the center and plants a tree!

4 If a player can't avoid landing on a black square, his/her environment suffers an ecological disaster. All that player's pyramids must be removed, but any plants may stay.

5 If a player lands on the same square as another piece, he/she may take pyramids from the other player's environment.

6 The winner is the first player to plant all four plants in his/her environment corner.

Most plants change with the seasons. When there is plenty of sun and rain, plants grow fast, putting out new shoots and leaves. In cold or dry seasons, they often appear to stop growing altogether. **Deciduous** trees have broad, flat leaves that give off a lot of water. They drop their leaves in autumn to conserve water and energy for the freezing winter months ahead.

spring

winter

You will need

wire – three different thicknesses
wire cutters
pliers
moss or foam rubber
paint
rubber cement

MAKE it WORK!

Making tree sculptures will show you how trees change with the seasons. Base your models on real trees if you can. You might even take photos of a tree to help you. Look carefully at the way trees' branches gradually get narrower and divide.

1 Start by winding several thick pieces of wire together to form the trunk and main branches of the tree. You may have to use pliers to do this. And be careful because the wire can be sharp.

2 Onto the main branches, attach a number of branches made from medium-weight wire. To those, attach twigs made from thin wire.

autumn

summer

◀ Ask an adult to help you cut the wire into short lengths to make your trees.

3 Make three more trees in the same way. Paint the winter and autumn trees a dark color. Paint the twigs on the spring and summer trees green.

4 Look around for tiny-leafed mosses or creeping plants to use for the leaves. If you cannot find any, use tiny pieces of foam rubber. This will not look quite the same as using real leaves, but it will give the same effect.

5 Stick a few leaves onto the spring tree and dab them with yellow paint. Stick plenty of leaves onto the summer tree and dab them with dark green paint. Dab the autumn leaves with red or orange paint and scatter a few around the base of the tree, as if they had fallen off.

Not every place in the world has four seasons. In the tropics, close to the Equator, it is hot year-round. There are just two seasons: the dry season and the wet one.

The biggest of all plants are trees. They have thick, woody stems which divide into branches. If you look closely at the way a tree's branches divide, you will start to notice a pattern. Each species of tree has a distinctive shape.

MAKE it WORK!

Look at the shapes of the trees around you. Some trees are tall and narrow; others are wide and round. Although most trees have green leaves, there is a lot of variety in the shades of green. Find out about unusual trees by looking in books and magazines. Which trees grow together? Which ones stand alone? Try making your own poster board forest.

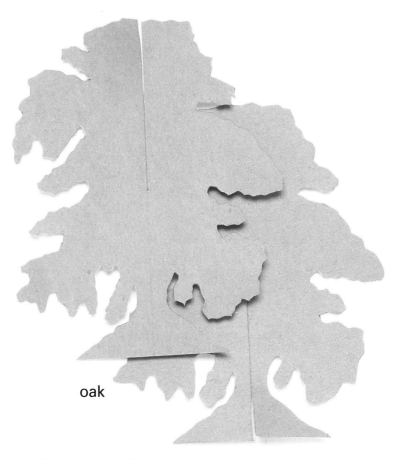

oak

You will need

graph paper	yard-length ruler
tracing paper	X-Acto knife
large sheets of paper	yard-length
large pieces of poster board	pencil

1 Draw the outline of a tree on graph paper. You may need to practice on scratch paper first to make your tree shape really accurate.

2 Trace your drawing onto poster board and cut it out with an X-Acto knife. Please ask an adult to help you use the knife. Trace it again and cut out an identical tree.

The world needs trees because, like all plants, they use up carbon dioxide and give out oxygen. Trees help to protect the balance of gases in the earth's atmosphere.

Lombardy poplar   North American ash

3 Cut a slit from the top of one tree shape to the middle, and from the bottom of the other to the middle. Slot them together.

4 Find out what trees grow near the tree you have made and make some more models. Then place them all together to make a model forest.

▼ To make giant trees, draw big squares on a large sheet of paper. Copy the lines from each square of your original drawing into the big squares. Transfer the outline onto big pieces of poster board, and slot together as before.

The trunk of a tree is made up of a complex system of cells: storage cells; strong supporting cells; and **sap** cells that carry water and nutrients to every part of the tree. The trunk is protected by the bark that surrounds it. Bark is made up of dead cells and varies in texture and thickness from tree to tree. Some barks are thick and deeply ridged; others are paper-thin and smooth. As a tree grows, the bark splits and forms cracks where mosses grow and beetles and spiders find shelter.

MAKE it WORK!

In order to compare and contrast the different textures and appearances of bark, do a series of bark rubbings: Label them with the type of tree and the date on which the rubbings were made. Then compare.

You will need

thick poster board
crayons
hole punch
ring fasteners
colored paper
masking tape

1 When you go outside to do your bark rubbing, take sheets of colored paper, tape, and crayons with you.

2 Inspect the trunk of the tree to find an interesting area of bark and tape your paper over it. Masking tape is the best kind of tape to use, as it sticks to bark. You will be able to peel it off later without ruining your paper.

3 Now rub the paper with a crayon. Soon the pattern of the bark will emerge. Rub gently, building up the color gradually; otherwise the paper might tear.

4 Once back from your field trip, file and catalog your findings. Make a folder using two pieces of stiff poster board and two ring fasteners. Cut out the clearest rubbings to go on file. Now label the rubbings, date them, punch holes in the sides and file them. You can also take rubbings of leaves and catalog them in the same way.

Tree bark is very useful. From the bark of the pine tree, for instance, a substance called tannin is extracted. Tannin is used to turn animal skins into leather. The bark of the willow tree gives us aspirin, which is used in medicines, and the bark of the cork oak gives us bottle corks and cork tiles.

Leaves make food for the plant. To make food, leaves need water, carbon dioxide, and sunlight. The process of making food is called **photosynthesis.** The result is a kind of sugary starch that is fed to all parts of the plant as sap. Photosynthesis takes place in the spongy layer of cells inside the leaf. The protective surface of the leaf allows air, water, and sap to flow through its veins. The green in leaves comes from **chlorophyll,** which is necessary for the food-making process.

▼ **Leaf box** Cut out a cube of Styrofoam and, using pins made from sharpened twigs, pin big leaves all around it. Another idea is to cut out a ball of Styrofoam and cover it with circular leaves such as nasturtium leaves.

MAKE it WORK!

Some leaves are a pale, golden green; others are a dark coppery red. Some leaves are soft and thick; others are hard and shiny. Make some leaf sculptures using different kinds of leaves. Here are a few ideas to get you going. You might want to photograph the results or just watch the leaves dry and change color.

You will need

Styrofoam	construction paper
leaves	blunt needle
sharpened twigs	thread or fishline
toothpicks	tape

◄ Leaf forest Collect some different colored leaves. Tape each leaf to the end of a toothpick. Poke the sticks into a sheet of construction paper and secure underneath with tape.

► Leaf hanging Use a blunt needle and some thick thread or fishline to string a collection of leaves together. Hang them from a shelf or from the ceiling and watch their colors change.

▼ Fern of ferns The fern shape below has been made from different sizes of fern leaf. You could make a giant oak-leaf shape out of oak leaves or an ivy-leaf shape from ivy leaves.

Ferns usually grow in damp, shady places. They are among the oldest types of plant found on the earth.

The shapes of leaves are even more varied than their colors are. Some are flat and wide, some are narrow and "needlelike", and others are thick. Flowers come in all different shapes, too. They range from enormous blooms to elegant trumpet-shapes and tiny, dainty flower heads. The varied shapes of flowers and leaves help them survive in each of their chosen environments.

You will need

leaves and flowers	paintbrush
paper	roller
thick paint	newspaper

gerbera

piggyback plant

poplar

laurel

fern

a compound leaf

a lobed leaf

▲ Remember to label your prints with the names of plants you have used.

daisy

MAKE it WORK!

Make a collection of prints of all sorts of leaves and flowers. Can you think of reasons why different leaves have different shapes?

1 Use a large paintbrush to cover the underside of a leaf with a thin layer of thick paint.

2 Place the leaf paintside down on a piece of paper and cover it with newspaper.

3 Gently rub over the newspaper with a roller to press the ink onto the paper beneath.

4 To make prints from flower heads, just coat them with paint and press them firmly down onto the paper with your hand.

Leaves are divided into three main groups: simple leaves, which have just one blade; lobed leaves, which have deep indentations; and compound leaves, which look like several leaves attached to one stalk.

Plants are an important source of food. We eat **fruits**, which are basically seedpods, as well as many different parts of vegetable plants. For example, we eat carrots and turnips, which are roots, broccoli, which is a flower, asparagus, which is a stem, and spinach, which is leaves.

MAKE it WORK!

Take a closer look at some of the different fruits and vegetables we eat. Look at the different textures. Some are very dense and dry, while others are juicy. Make a collection of fruit and vegetable prints.

You will need

white paper   knife
thick paint
paintbrush
fruits and vegetables

1 Ask an adult to help you slice through a fruit or vegetable at its fattest point, either across (horizontally) or down (vertically) – whichever you think will make the most interesting impression.

2 Cover the slice of fruit or vegetable you are going to print with a thin layer of thick paint.

3 Press the painted slice down firmly on the paper. Try to press down one time only, to avoid making any smudges.

4 Leave your prints to dry; then label them and put them in a folder. (See pages 24–25). Never eat fruit and vegetables that have been painted.

broccoli

pepper

lemon

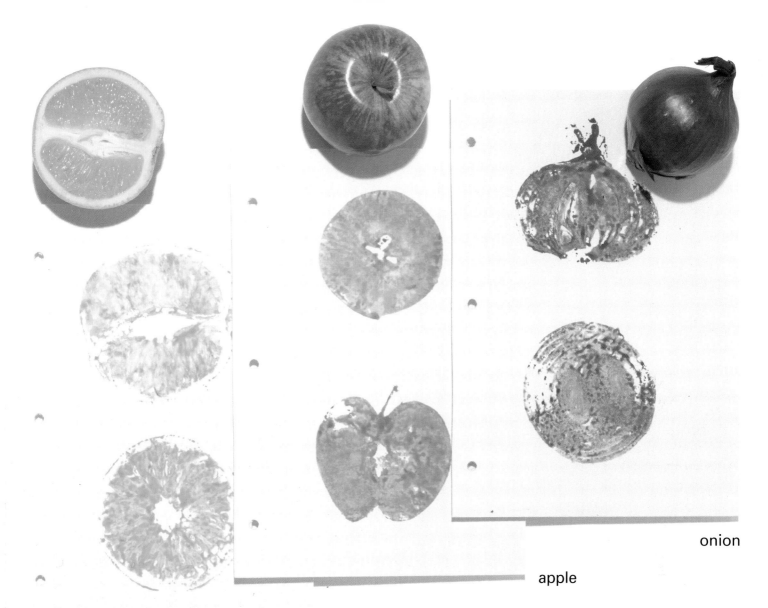

onion

apple

orange

Some animals eat only plants — they are called **herbivores**. Some animals eat only meat — they are called **carnivores**. Some animals, and most humans, eat both plants and meat and are known as **omnivores**. However, plants are vital to the diet of every living thing. If there were no plants, herbivores would not have enough to eat and they would eventually die out. If there were no herbivores, the carnivores would also have no meat to eat. Thus without plants, there could be no human or animal life on earth at all.

FRUITS

If you look at flowers closely, you will find that they all have the same four basic parts: the outer **sepals**, which enclose the flower as it grows; the **corolla**, or petals; the **stamen**, small stalks that hold sacs of **pollen** grains; and the **carpels**, the parts where seeds grow.

You will need

poster board	thick colored paper
flowers	waterproof glue
X-Acto knife	graph paper

MAKE it WORK!

Make some model flowers copied from real ones you see in a garden or in photographs.

2 Cut out the petaled pentagon in one piece. Do the same for the other two. Glue the small one to the middle one and the middle one to the big one.

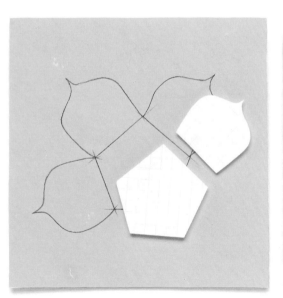

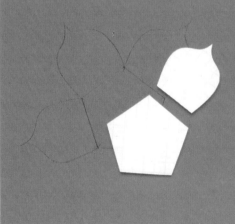

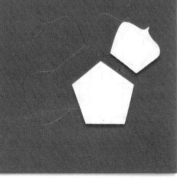

1 Draw a pentagon on a piece of graph paper, and then draw a petal shape with a base that fits onto one of the five sides of the pentagon. Repeat this process two times, each time making the pentagon a little smaller. Then cut out the petal shape to use as a pattern for more petals.

3 Cut and fold a piece of poster board to make stamens and carpels for your flower.

4 Fold up the petals and then place the flower in water. You can dry out these flowers and use them again.

*Flowers are the **reproductive** part of the plant. They contain both the male cells, called the pollen, and the female cells, called the ovules or eggs. The ovules are inside the carpel. Reproduction takes place when pollen gets inside the carpel, and fertilizes an ovule.*

Most flowers are large and brightly colored. The colors attract insects, which feed on the sweet nectar inside the flowers. Some flowers have patterns that cannot be seen by the human eye but that are quite clear to insects.

MAKE it WORK!

Make a collection of flowers and then press them in a flower press. Never pick wildflowers unless you can see lots of similar flowers nearby. And even then, only pick a few!

You will need

two pieces of wood	poster board
four long screws	rubber cement
thick cardboard	tissue paper
four washers and nuts	blotting paper

Ask an adult to help you cut two pieces of wood and drill holes in each of the four corners. Cut the cardboard and blotting paper the same size as the wood. Cut off the corners so that the screws do not pierce the cardboard and paper.

▶ Lay cardboard on the bottom piece of wood. Place a piece of blotting paper on top. Arrange a flower on the paper and cover it with another piece of blotting paper and cardboard. Repeat until the pile just fits between the screws.

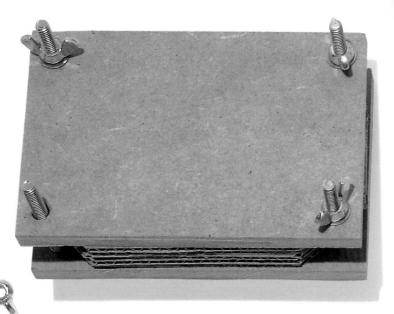

▲ Place the second piece of wood on top and screw down firmly. Leave for a month. The longer you leave the flowers, the less they will fade.

purple heather

roses

pink larkspur

Dried Flowers

Some flowers can be dried by hanging them upside down. To do this, tie the flowers by their stems and hang them upsidedown from the ceiling. Some will take a week to dry out and others, much longer. Some flowers lose their color when they are dried. Experiment with different types of flowers to see which ones work best.

Many plants need the help of insects to bring the ovules and pollen together to make a seed. Insects such as bees are attracted by the bright colors of the flowers and by the sweet nectar. A bee enters a flower for a drink of nectar and leaves carrying pollen. When it enters the next flower, the pollen is rubbed off the bee's body and onto the ovules of the new flower, so that the ovule is fertilized.

▲ Arrange your dried flowers on thin poster board, and when you are happy with the position of the stem and leaves, stick them down with rubber cement. You could place tissue paper between the cards to protect the flowers.

When seeds have developed inside the plant, it is time for them to leave and start a new life of their own. Some plants just drop their seeds nearby, but most try to spread their seeds as far apart as possible. Some seeds, like those of the dandelion, have parachutes so they can be carried with the wind. The water lily's seeds have built-in life rafts so they can float on water. Some spiky seeds, such as burrs, attach themselves to animals' fur. Other delicious seeds, such as berries, are eaten by animals and passed through their bodies as waste, to be deposited in some far-off shrubbery.

lemon

pips

stone

peach

walnut

nut

▲ Split open some fruits to see what their seeds are like. A nut is a seed too—its shell is called the hard fruit of a nut tree or plant.

◄ **Spore Prints**
Some plants, like mushrooms and toadstools, do not have seeds. Instead, they have **spores**. These spores are contained beneath the cap. To make a spore print, carefully cut the stalk off of an open mushroom. Place the cap, open side down, on a piece of white paper. Leave overnight; then carefully lift off the mushroom. The spores will have fallen out of the mushroom cap, forming a print.

*Seeds do not begin to grow as soon as they reach the ground. They remain **dormant** until the conditions are right, which in most cases is when spring arrives. But some seeds, such as those of desert plants, may wait for years!*

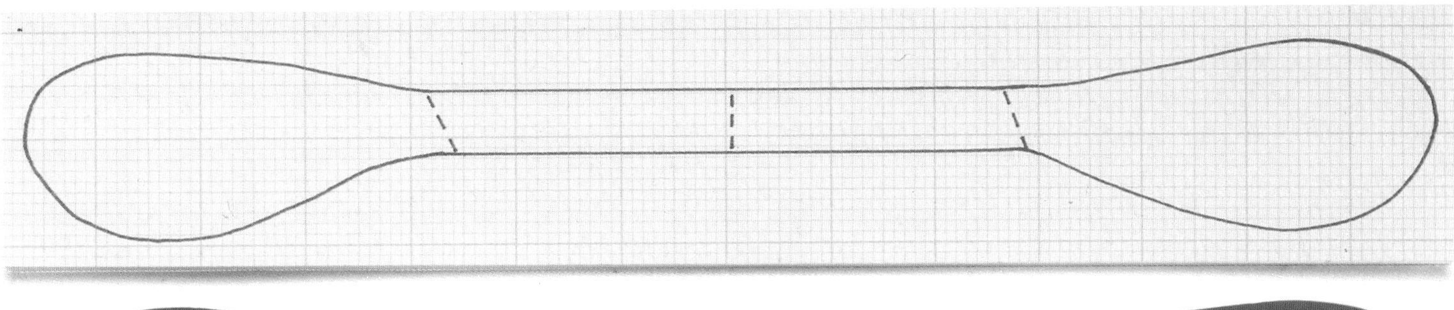

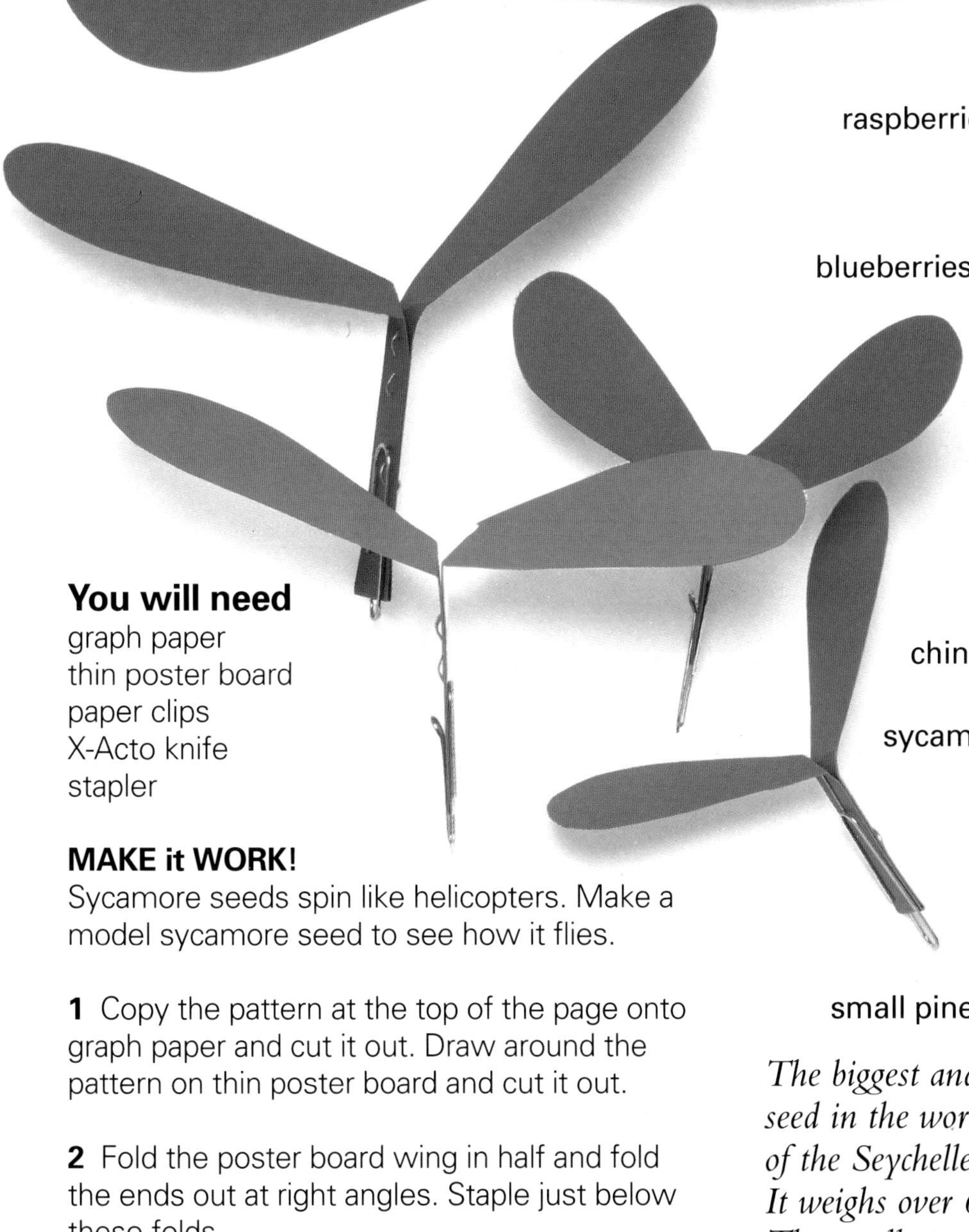

raspberries

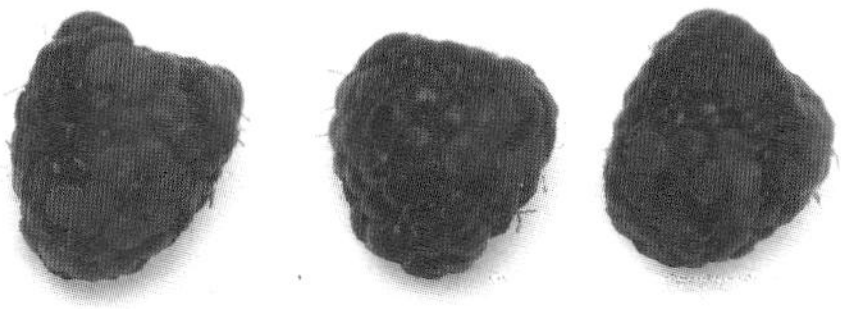

blueberries

chinese lanterns

sycamore seeds

small pine cones

You will need

graph paper
thin poster board
paper clips
X-Acto knife
stapler

MAKE it WORK!

Sycamore seeds spin like helicopters. Make a model sycamore seed to see how it flies.

1 Copy the pattern at the top of the page onto graph paper and cut it out. Draw around the pattern on thin poster board and cut it out.

2 Fold the poster board wing in half and fold the ends out at right angles. Staple just below these folds.

3 Attach a paper clip to the bottom of the helicopter. This is the "seed", which balances the wings. Now throw your sycamore seed high in the air and watch it spin to earth.

The biggest and heaviest seed in the world is that of the Seychelles coconut. It weighs over 66 lbs. The smallest seeds are orchid seeds. Three million of them would weigh only .04 oz.

Even after plants die, they are still very important to the environment. Decaying plants return their nutrients to the soil, making it rich and fertile for the next generation. Plants begin to **decompose** as soon as they are picked. The mold spores that cause decay creep into the plant as its protective layer of skin starts to break down; and multiply very quickly. As food decays, it shrivels and becomes lighter, because the mold spores are eating it up. Mold spores are **microorganisms**, which means they are so small they cannot be seen without a microscope.

You will need

fruits and vegetables	glue
camera or colored pencils	paper
brown poster board	X-Acto knife

Be very careful with decayed food! Never taste it and wash your hands after touching it.

MAKE it WORK!

The best way to study decay is to watch it happen! Cut up some fruits and vegetables and leave them out to spoil. Try leaving pieces of food in different places to test the length of time they take to decay. Leave some on a warm windowsill, some in a cool cupboard and some outside. Take photos of them every few days or draw pictures of them, and keep a record of your findings in a special file box like the one on the right.

1 Attach your photos or drawings to cards. Cut out dividers to place between them.

orange

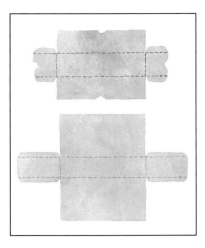

gluing and folding

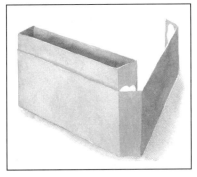

reinforcing the box

box and lid shapes

2 To make your file box, copy the shapes on the right onto smooth brown poster board. Cut along the solid lines and score-(notch) along the dotted ones. Fold along the scored lines and glue.

3 Glue an additional piece of poster board around the box, leaving a gap of about an inch at the top. This will help the lid sit firmly on the box.

▼ The tabs on your dividers should be in different positions so you can read them easily.

Bacteria are microorganisms that cause diseases like fevers and sore throats. There was no cure for such diseases until 1928, when British scientist Sir Alexander Fleming noticed mold growing on a laboratory dish of bacteria. The bacteria around the mold had been killed off by the same kind of mold that grows on cheese! Fleming had discovered penicillin, a medicine that has saved many people's lives.

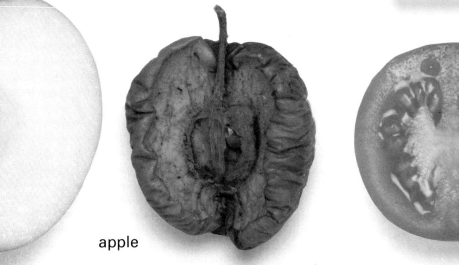

apple

tomato

All specimens rot over time unless they are preserved in some way. The only reason we know about the plants that grew on earth millions of years ago is because many species were **fossilized**. A living plant fell into mud, leaving its mark in the soft earth. Fresh layers of mud trapped the plant, and the mud gradually hardened into rock, with the imprint of the plant still there, in vivid detail. Plant fossils, such as imprints of ferns and mosses, can be found in all kinds of rocks. Others, such as tree roots, are found in underground mines.

▲ Can you make out the fossil of a plant inside this lump of coal?

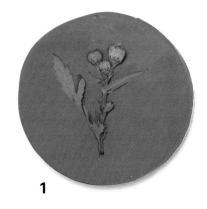

1

2

MAKE it WORK!
You can make your own "fossil," a permanent record of even your most delicate specimen, using soft modeling clay and plaster of paris. A three-dimensional model will allow you to examine the shape and texture of your specimen long after the actual object has decayed.

You will need
plaster of paris
modeling clay
roller
poster board
paper clips
plant specimen

1 Roll out a ball of modeling clay so that it is flat and smooth. Place the specimen on the clay and press it down into the clay with your fingers or the roller.

2 Carefully pull the specimen away from the modeling clay.

Do you know what coal is made of? It is the result of millions of years of rotting plants and trees that sank into the earth and were later buried by more earth. The weight of these upper layers gradually squeezed all the moisture out of the rotting vegetation and pressed it into a solid mass of peat. The peat eventually hardened and became coal. Sometimes you can look at a piece of coal and see fossils of the original seedpods and roots. All the energy that was in those plants so long ago has turned into a substance called **carbon,** which still gives us energy today.

▶ You can display your plaster casts in a shallow-sided box filled with clean sawdust to stop them from getting knocked over or chipped. You also can paint the plaster casts to show the colors of the original specimens.

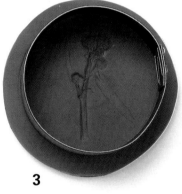

3

4

5

3 Make a circle from poster board and use a paper clip to hold it in place. Press the circle into the clay so it encircles the print.

4 Prepare a small amount of plaster of paris and pour it into the poster board ring.

5 Leave the mold undisturbed overnight so that the plaster hardens properly; then remove the clay and the poster board ring.

4

5

You may have noticed that if you spill beet juice on a white T-shirt, it doesn't wash out. Beet juice is a natural dye. Today, most clothes are dyed with chemical dyes, but before these were invented, people had been using plants to bring color into their lives for thousands of years.

MAKE it WORK!

Try extracting dye from onion skins and using it to tie-dye a square of cotton or a T-shirt.

1 Peel the skin gently from a large brown onion: Put the skins into a piece of muslin, tie it up, and put it into a pan of cold water.

2 Wet the fabric and put it in the pan. Bring the water to a gentle simmer and keep it simmering until the fabric is the color you want it. It will take from twenty minutes to three hours. Stir regularly.

3 Lift the fabric out of the pan with a wooden spoon and rinse in clean warm water until no more color runs out. Allow to dry naturally.

You will need

large saucepan
onion skins
muslin
wooden spoon
marbles and pebbles
 in assorted sizes
white butcher's string
strainer
glass jars

Be careful!

Pans of boiling water are dangerous. Make sure your pan is big enough to hold the fabric and the water without spilling. Never try to boil water without an adult around to help you.

Tie-dyeing

The principle behind tie-dyeing is to stop the dye from getting to certain parts of the fabric in order to make interesting patterns.

1 For a fairly free, random effect, just tie a knot in the center of the fabric. The looser the knot, the greater the spread of the dye. You can tie just one knot or a series of knots.

2 For a striped pattern, roll the fabric into a loose sausage and tie string tightly around it. Tie string at regular intervals if you want regular stripes, or in varying spaces if you want something more random.

3 For a circle pattern, put a pebble or marble in the center, fold the cloth around it, and secure it with string. You can use a series of marbles of the same size or you can vary the pattern by using an assortment of pebbles.

Keeping the dye

You can use your dye again and again, as long as you keep it free from vegetable matter, which would quickly spoil. Even though you have tied up your plants, roots, or skins securely in a muslin pouch, little particles will inevitably escape. When the dye has cooled, remove the muslin pouch and pour the dye through a strainer into clean glass jars with screw-top lids. Label the jars and keep them in a dark cupboard, as exposure to sunlight will cause the dyes to fade. As soon as the dyes start to look cloudy, throw them away.

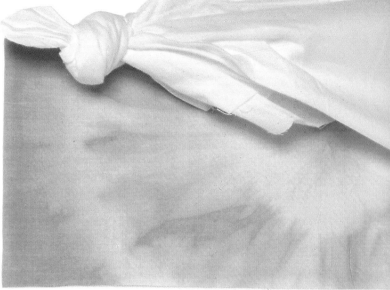

a random effect

striped pattern

circle pattern

Experiment with color

Now that you know how to extract dyes, try the process with different plants, roots, and leaves. You will notice that results differ depending on which fabric you use. Cotton will turn out paler than wool, because wool is more absorbent than cotton.

Some natural dyes are not colorfast, which means they will gradually wash out of the fabric if a substance called a **mordant** is not added. The mordant combines with the dye to make the color enter the fibers of the fabric and produce a color that will not fade.

▶ All the plants shown here will produce dyes that are naturally colorfast. Follow the directions on the previous page, remembering to put the plant, root, skins, or powder into a muslin pouch. For the turmeric powder (a spice used in Indian cooking) you may need a double layer of muslin. Note: The color of the fabrics dyed with the yellow flowers of the goldenrod are in fact more green than yellow.

Among the most popular dyes are the intense yellow ones obtained from the stamens of the saffron crocus, the dark blue ones that come from the Indian indigo plant (which we know better as the color of blue jeans), and the orange-red of the henna plant, which is used today as a hair dye.

The ancient Phoenicians discovered that certain spiny snail shells, when crushed, produced a beautiful purple dye. It was very costly, and with the Romans in particular, the color became associated with wealth and power. To this day, kings and queens wear ceremonial robes of deep purple.

tea bags or loose tea

turmeric powder

avocado skins

beet juice

onion skins

goldenrod

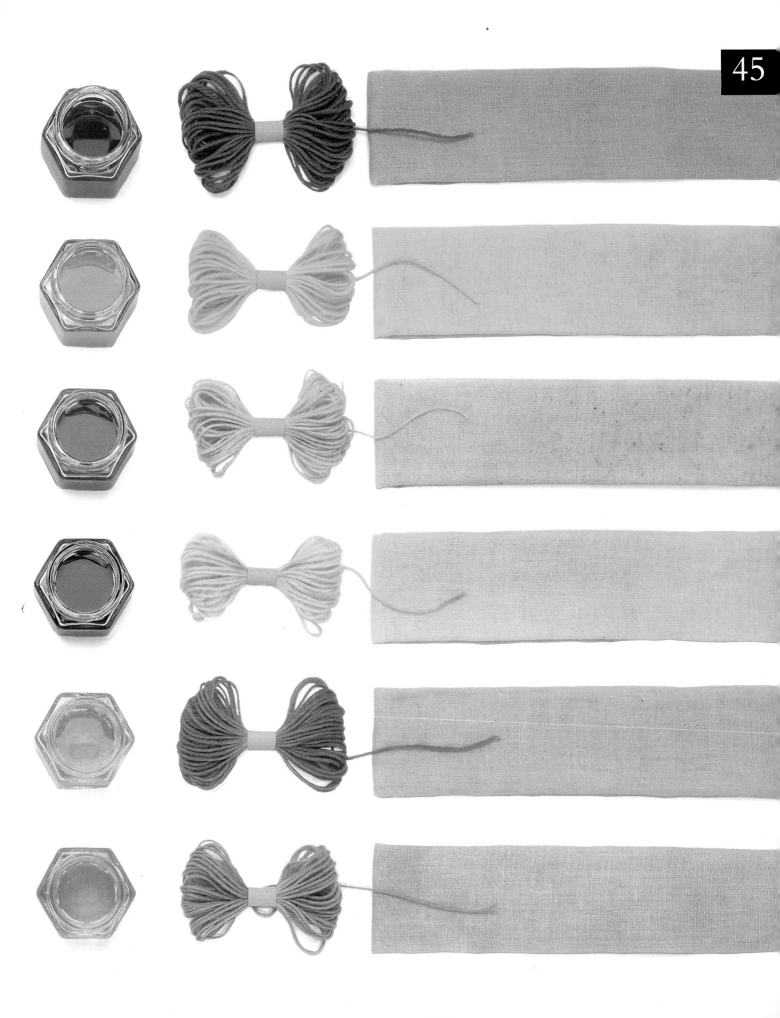

Algae Simple plants that live in water or damp places.

Bacteria Microscopic plants. Many bacteria cause disease.

Biology The study of all living things.

Botany The study of plants.

Calibrated If a stick is calibrated, it is marked out so that it can be used for measuring. A ruler is a calibrated piece of wood or plastic.

Carbon A substance that exists in many different forms and is found in all plants. Coal is a kind of carbon, made from the decomposed remains of plants and animals that died millions of years ago.

Carbon dioxide A colorless gas with no smell. It is an important part of the air that we breathe.

Carnivores Meat-eating animals.

Carpels The female parts of flowers where the seeds are produced.

Cataloging Cataloging is the careful organizing, listing, and storage of information, so that it can be found again easily.

Chlorophyll A chemical found in the stems and leaves of plants, which gives them their green color. It takes in energy from the sun and helps convert it into food for the plant.

Conifers Plants that grow their seeds in cones, such as fir trees, pines, and cedars.

Corolla The rings of petals that form a flower.

Data Information that has been gathered in an organized way.

Deciduous Deciduous plants lose their leaves once a year, in the autumn.

Decompose To decay, or rot. Dead plants decompose with the help of bacteria.

Dormant Inactive, or asleep. When plants are dormant, they are not growing.

Environment The conditions that surround a plant or animal. Every living thing needs a particular environment (for instance, the right kind of soil, food, and climate) to survive.

Evaporate When a liquid evaporates, it changes into a gas. For example, when water evaporates, it becomes steam, or water vapor.

Experiments Tests done to discover answers or to confirm assumptions.

Ferns Plants that grow in moist, wooded areas. They have fronds rather than leaves.

Fossil Fossils are stones containing the imprint or remains of a plant or animal that lived in prehistoric times.

Fruit Fruit is the edible part of a plant.

Fungi Fungi are plants that do not flower and do not contain the chemical chlorophyll. The commonest fungi are mushrooms and toadstools.

Herbivores Plant-eating animals.

Hormones Hormones are chemicals found in every living thing. They are what make plants and animals grow.

Lichens Simple plants that grow in clumps like moss. They do not need soil but can grow on rocks or the barks of trees.

Microorganisms Plants or animals that are too small to be seen by the human eye. Bacteria are microorganisms.

Mordant A chemical that combines with dye to produce a color that will not fade.

Mosses Tiny, simple plants that reproduce from spores rather than from seeds.

Omnivores Animals that eat plants and meat.

Photosynthesis Photosynthesis is the process by which plants use sunlight to change water and carbon dioxide into food.

Pollen A powdery substance, which contains the male cells needed for a plant to reproduce.

Reproductive The part of the plant that makes new life, which in many plants is the flower.

Sap A sugary liquid that plants make to feed themselves. Sap is made from sunlight, water, and air by the process of photosynthesis.

Scientist Someone who studies the world in a systematic way, to try and understand how it works.

Sepal The outer part of a flower bud.

Species A group of animals that appear to be the same and behave in a similar way.

Specimen A sample of a plant or animal that scientists use for experiments.

Spores Spores are single plant cells that are neither male nor female.

Stamen The stalk part of the flower that hold pollen grains.

Theory An idea that tries to explain something. Scientific theories usually have to be proved by experiments before they are said to be true.